Cherokee Recipes, Cooking Tips & Lore

Dean Tackett

Copyright © 1996

All Rights Reserved

No part of this book may be reproduced, copied or distributed in any printed or electronic form without permission of author.

Cherokee Press
Tulsa, Oklahoma
Printed in the United States of America

ISBN: 0-9657331-0-6
ISBN-13: 978-0-9657331-0-6
EAN: 9780965733106

Visit us at http://cherokeerecipes.com

Cherokee
ORIGINAL

Recipes,

Cooking Tips & Lore

Written by

Dean Tackett

Publisher & Editor

Table of Contents

About This Book..................1
The Sacred Fire...................2
The Green Corn Ceremony….....3
Maize Recipes - Corn.............4
The Corn Drink
Dried Corn
Skillet Corn
Maize, the history of Corn…......5
Cherokee Corn Cob Jelly…….....6
Corn Bread
Corn Bread Dressing……………7
Corn Pones
Selu, Mother of Corn…………8
Fresh Corn Pudding…………10
Crackling Bread
Buttermilk Corn Bread……..11
Corn Pudding Casserole….....12
Tangy Chilled Corn Chowder

Corn Shuck Bread............13
Walnut Corn Hominy....................…14
Hominy Hash
Pork Chops and Hominy.....15
Fried Hominy…….….…...16
Hominy Soup
Hominy with Rotel…..…....17
Hominy Casserole
Pumpkins & Squash……....18
Dried Pumpkin
Dried Winter Squash
Cream of Pumpkin Soup…..19
Pumpkin Bread
Pumpkin Soup…….……...20
Baked Pumpkin…....………21
Cream of Squash Soup
Fried Squash Blossoms……22
Baked Summer Squash
Party Squash………...…….23

Kanati, the Game Hunter……..24
Wild Rice Soup
       And Vegetables……….…...25
Cabbage Soup
Cream of Cucumber Soup….....26
Cherokee Pecan Soup………...27
Oatmeal Soup
Black Bean Soup……….………28
Cherokee Pepper Pot Soup…...29
Fish Soup
Turkey Bone Soup……….……..30
Peanut Soup
Mushroom and Potato Soup….31
Potato Soup…………….………32
Cream of Cauliflower Soup
Mint and Nut Soup…….……….33
Tortilla Soup
Mock Turtle Soup……….………34
Cherokee Bean Balls….……....35
Fried Tomato Pones

Wild Rice Casserole...............36
Leather Britches.................37
Wild Greens......................38
Poke, Wild Onions & Other
    Wild Greens..................39
Garlic Tomato....................40
Sweet Potato Cakes
Baked Sweet Potatoes
Cherokee Mixit...................41
Tomato Soup Salad
Mayan Salad......................42
Cumin Dressing
Spinach Salad with Chutney
    Dressing.....................43
Chutney Dressing
Hot Green Bean Salad.............44
Fried Okra Salad
Black-eyed Pea Salad.............45
Cucumber Salad

Tossed Fresh Fruit Salad……..46
Orange Mayonnaise Dressing
Watercress Salad
Cole Slaw………………..……..47
Red Onion Marinade
Dill Pickle Salad……...……..48
Poppy Seed Dressing
Spoon Bread………………….49
Buttermilk Biscuits
Cherokee Fry Bread………….50
Fry Bread
Indian Herb Dressing………...51
Cold Beef Salad……………...52
Fried Green Tomatoes
Fried Mushrooms
Sourdough Biscuits…………..53
Sourdough Starter
Chestnut Bread
Carrot Bread…………………54
Cherokee Huckleberry Bread

Bean Bread……………........55
Blue Corn Muffins
Homemade Cornmeal
 Tortillas………………….…...56
Persimmon Bread
Blueberry Wild Rice
 Muffins……………….……..57
Strawberry Bread
Bread Stuffing…..……………58
Spoon Bread
Chipped Beef in
 Mushroom Sauce………....59
Drip Beef
Paprika Beef……………....…60
Venison Steak
Roast Venison
Fried Rabbit……………..……61
Batter Fried Frog Legs
Cerviche

Herbed Chicken……………...62
Chicken Breast Casserole
Breast of Chicken with
   Wild Rice………………....63
Venison Stew……………....64
Country Fried Squirrel
Squirrel Stew
Hickory Nut Pie…………....65
Baked Indian Pudding
Pear Pudding………….….…66
Sweet Potato Pudding
Pecan Balls……………….....67
Baked Apricots
Cherokee Persimmon Cake
Grape Dumplings……….….68

About This Book

On The Cover:
Original
Painting
Contributed by
Mars Biggoose
"A Good Friend"

The "Made by American Indians" trademark is a registered trademark with the U.S. Patent Office. Cherokee Publications has been authorized to use this trademark by the Intertribal Agriculture Council. The guidelines for authorization have been met by Cherokee Publications for this cookbook.

The Cookbook is the first in a series of five cookbooks to be published, one for each of the Five Civilized Tribes. The recipes in this book are a mixture of original recipes and the recipes of today's Cherokee household. Cherokee Publications would like to thank the Five Civilized Tribes Museum, in Muskogee, for allowing the publication of some of their recipes in this Cookbook. These recipes were taken from the *Pow Wow Chow.* You may find additional recipes from the *Pow Wow Chow* cookbook in the Five Civilized Tribes Museum located in the old Union Indian Agency in Muskogee. It is our recommendation that you visit the Museum for an interesting tour of Indian culture.

The stories contained within this cookbook are told from days long ago. We sincerely hope this book will be an enjoyment for your appetite, your body and your soul.

The Sacred Fire

The Sacred Fire was brought to Oklahoma by the Cherokees along the Trail of Tears. Unlike some of the other Southeastern tribes, the Cherokees always believed the spirit of the fire to be feminine. The fire and the Sun were both represented as an old woman. They held the old woman in great esteem and honor. They would always feed her a little bit of whatever they were cooking.

To treat the Old Woman of the Fire with disrespect by failing to give her a portion of your food or putting something unclean into the fire might make her angry and she would turn into a whippoorwill or an owl and that would bring you bad luck.

Each year at the beginning of the Green Corn Ceremony all fires in the village were put out. A new Sacred Fire was started with a fire drill at the end of the Green Corn Ceremony by the priests. All new fires were started from this new central Sacred Fire.

The Green Corn Ceremony

The Green Corn Ceremony was a celebration of the new harvest each year. It was a time of thanksgiving and purification for the coming year. It was a time when the corn was ripe and ready to eat, a time for starting a new year. The people would prepare for weeks for the celebration. New clothes, baskets and pottery were made to replace the old. At the beginning of the four day ceremony their houses would be cleared of all rubbish, the people would visit eahc other settling all old quarrels and grievances. Old clothes and pottery were destroyed and replaced with new things. The old fires were put out and rekindled from the new Sacred Fire. For four days they feasted on green corn, which represented fertility of the new corn crop.

Maize Recipes — Corn

the Corn Drink

This corn drink was always available in Cherokee homes and the variations of ingredients and preparation differ from family to family. Here are the basics, but be creative, in a heavy skillet parch about 1 cup dry corn over low heat. Stirring constantly, until golden brown. Place parched corn into a mortar and pound into a coarse meal. In a Large pot cook meal with 3 cups water for about 30 minutes, add more water if mixture begins to get too thick, salt to taste. Experiment by adding nuts, beans, fresh pork or even some wood ashes for a smoked Flavor.

Dried Corn

Boil roasting ears of corn for 10 minutes, leaving the shuck on. Cool, pull back the shucks but leave them attached to the cob. Hang in a dry space for about 2 weeks or until corn is dried. Shell off kernels and store in airtight bags. Dried corn can be used in several recipes or simply placed in saucepan, covered with water and boiled until tender, about 2 to 3 hours. Salt and pepper to taste. Also add butter if you wish.

Skillet

Place 1 pint of Fresh kernels into skillet with 1/2 cup water, 1/2 cup shortening, I tbsp sugar, salt and pepper to taste. Fry over low heat for 1 to 10 minutes.

Maize

In most parts of the world, oats, barley and wheat are commonly referred to as corn. What we know as corn is really "maize". The first Europeans to come here called maize, "Indian Corn". So we now know it as "corn".

Maize came to the North American tribes through Central and South America where it has been used as food by those tribes for thousands of years. Some researchers believe that the people of the American continents were planting their own crops nearly 9,000 years ago. The maize or corn that we know today looks very little like the maize that has been found by researchers. The early maize was little more than a grass with a few kernels, but no cob. Cultivation by the earliest Native American ancestors developed this glasslike, wild maize into a plant that would produce corn on a cob which produced more and better food than the precious wild maize brought forth. With the development of cultivation of maize, along with squash, beans, and gourds, the people could settle into villages and stay longer. So, along with the development of maize came a settling of the people for longer periods, more permanent dwellings and longer lasting relationships among themselves as a tribe.

Cherokee Corn Cob Jelly

12 ears fresh corn
4 cups water
4 cups sugar
1 3 fluid ounce package
   Liquid fruit pectin

Cut kernels from cob and save kernels for other recipes Boil cobs covered in water for 12 to 15 minutes. Remove cobs and strain liquid. Add enough water to bring strained liquid to 3 cups. Bring liquid to a boil in saucepan stirring in sugar until dissolved. Stir in pectin and cook 1 minute Remove from heat, skim and place in sterile jars.

Corn Bread

1 cup corn meal
1/2 cup flour
2 tsp baking powder
1 tbsp sugar
2 cups milk
1/4 cup melted shortening or oil
1 egg, beaten

Mix all ingredients thoroughly and pour into greased, heated pan. Bake at 450° until brown, about 30 minutes.

Corn bread Dressing

4 cups cornbread, crumbled
2 cups biscuits, crumbled
1 large onion, finely chopped
2 tsp sage
1 tsp salt
1/2 tsp pepper
1 cup chopped celery
2 cups chicken broth
2 eggs beaten

Mix corn bread and biscuit crumbs, onion, sage, salt and pepper. Mix well then add celery and mix thoroughly. Mix broth with eggs and pour broth over dry mixture. Put dressing in greased pan about 1 1/2 to 2 inches thick. Bake at 375° until browned on top.

Corn Pones

1 1/2 cups corn meal
1 1/2 tsp baking powder
1/2 tsp salt
3/4 cup water or milk
5 tbsp bacon drippings or corn oil

Combine dry ingredients in mixing bowl. Stir in water or milk with 3 tbsp bacon drippings. Spoon into greased heated skillet. Fry until browned on both sides.

Selu
Mother of Corn

The spirit' of the corn, according to legend, is provided by Selu, Mother or Corn. Selu lived at a time when corn was provided by the Maker, without work, through the magical powers given to Selu.

She lived with her husband and two sons in the mountain region. Selu would go to the storehouse everyday by herself and bring back a basket of corn.

Her two sons were very curious about this and being mischievous one day, decided to follow Selu to the storehouse. The storehouse, stood above the ground supported by four poles. After Selu entered the storehouse; the sons climbed up on the outside and dug a hole in the mud between the logs of the storehouse so they could peek inside.

There they saw the great mystery of Selu as she set the basket on the floor and began to shake herself. As she shook, corn began to fall off her body into the basket until it was full.

Later the boys discussed this curious matter hey derided that t h e i r mother, Selu, must be a witch.

Now this meant that Selu must be put to death, because all witches were put to death. Now, Selu could read the thoughts of her sons and gave them instructions for her body after they had put her to death. She told them that this would provide them with plenty of corn in the future.

Here are the instructions that Selu left her sons. "After you have killed me, clear a large piece of ground in front of the house and drag my body around in a circle inside the cleared ground, seven times, stay up all night and watch.

The boys did as Selu said except they only cleared seven small spots of ground and they only dragged her body twice in a circle. Where Selu's blood fell corn began to grow in those spots. Because the sons didn't follow Selu's instructions correctly, corn now must be planted and taken care of in order for it to grow, and still only grows in certain spots and not over the entire Earth.

Fresh Corn Pudding

6 to 8 ears fresh corn

1 egg, separated

2 tbsp sugar

1 tsp salt

3 tbsp butter, softened

1/2 cup milk

1 tsp vanilla extract

Cut corn from cob, scraping cob to remove pulp. Measure 3 cups of corn and pulp mixture. Combine corn, egg yolk, sugar, salt, butter, milk, and vanilla. Mix thoroughly. Beat egg white until stiff, fold into corn mixture. Place into greased baking dish. Bake at 350° for 30-40 minutes.

Crackling Bread

1 1/2 cups corn meal

2 tsp baking powder

2 cups buttermilk

1/2 tsp soda

1 egg, beaten

1 cup cracklings (see below)

Mix all ingredients and place in cake pan. Bake at 400° until corn bread is brown on top. For Cracklings When all the lard has been rendered from pork fat, the crunchy bits that are left are cracklings. You can make them by taking small pieces of fat from pork roast or chops and frying slowly until brown and crunchy. Do not allow grease to get hot enough to smoke.

Buttermilk Corn Bread

1 1/2 cup white corn meal

2 tsp baking powder

1/2 tsp baking soda

2 cups buttermilk

1/4 cup melted shortening or oil

1 egg, beaten

Mix all ingredients thoroughly and pour into greased, heated pan. Bake at 450° until brown, about 30 minutes.

Corn Fritters

1 cup self-rising flour

1 tsp. sugar

1 tsp. salt

1/2 tsp. pepper

2 eggs, beaten

1 1/2 cups fresh corn
   Cut from cob (3 ears)

1/2 cup milk

2 tbsp vegetable oil

Combine 1st 4 ingredients in large mixing bowl. Mix thoroughly, set aside.

Combine eggs, corn, milk & 2 tbsp vegetable oil, and mix well. Heat oil to 375°. Drop mixture by rounded spoon into hot oil until golden brown on each side. Drain on paper towel before serving.

Corn Pudding Casserole

1 can cream style corn
2 eggs beaten
1/2 cup milk
1/2 tsp salt
2 tsp flour
2 tbsp flour
2 tbsp melted butter
1/8 tsp pepper
1 small onion, finely diced
5 soda crackers, crumbled

Mix first 9 ingredients thoroughly in a mixing bowl. Pour into baking dish and sprinkle with cracker crumbs. Bake at 350° for 1 hour.

Tangy Chilled Corn Chowder

1 1/3 cups fresh corn, cooked and cut off cobs
1 qt. buttermilk
juice 1/2 lime
1/3 cup scallions cut into 1" shafts
salt
Fresh ground pepper
3 to 4 sprigs fresh dill

Boil corn in rapidly boiling water for 2 to 3 minutes. Combine corn and scallion shafts with buttermilk. Add lime juice, salt and pepper to taste. Chill for several hours. Serve garnished with dill sprigs.

Corn Shuck Bread

To prepare shucks for bread, take the shucks from ears of mature dry corn and wash thoroughly. Place in a pot and pour boiling water over them. Allow to soak until pliable.

3 cups corn meal

2 cups boiling water

1 tsp soda

Mix corn meal with soda thoroughly. Pour boiling water into mixture to make batter. Shape into oblong pones, about 3 inches long and 1 inch thick. Wrap in layers of corn husk and tie husk. Drop pones into rapidly boiling water for 20 to 30 minutes. Remove bread from water and serve.

Walnut Corn

1 can whole kernel corn

1 small package black walnuts

2 tbsp butter

Cook corn according to package directions, adding the black walnuts and butter. (Black walnuts may be substituted with other nuts, pecans, peanuts or hickory nuts will work.)

Hominy

Dried corn, removed from the cob, and soaked in hot water mixed with wood ashes is the method the Cherokee prepared Hominy. These methods were used before the Removal, by the Trail of Tears, to Indian Territory, which is now called Oklahoma. After soaking and beating with a stick the husks come off and the kernels puff up. The kernels are then boiled in fresh water until tender. Hominy meal was used to make batter for bread, fritters and pones. Bread was baked by putting loaves in a clay pot, then covered with another pot, and then covered with hot coals to bake.

A traditional method for preparing hominy is to take clean wood ashes (hardwoods such as oak or hickory are best) sifted and put into an iron kettle. (Aluminum is never used for making hominy) Cover with water and boil until the skin slips on the corn. Wash the skins and ashes away with plenty of fresh water. The hominy is ready for use. Hominy can be boiled with salt and bacon drippings or cooked with beans.

Hominy Hash

3 tbsp bacon drippings or corn oil
2 cups boiled hominy
2 green onions, sliced thin
4 eggs, beaten
Salt and pepper to taste

Sauté hominy and green onions in bacon drippings in hot skillet until lightly browned. Pour in eggs and season to taste. After eggs have set, turn mixture and allow to brown on other side. Serve with bacon and biscuits if you prefer.

Pork Chops and Hominy

4-6 pork chops (thick)
1 can mushroom soup (undiluted)
2 cups hominy
Salt and pepper to taste

In heavy skillet brown pork chops on both sides. Place hominy in bottom of casserole dish. Placed browned pork chops over hominy. Salt and pepper to taste. Pour mushroom soup over pork chops. Bake at 350° to 375° for 1 hour. Serve hot.

Fried Hominy

2 strips bacon
2 cups hominy
2 or 3 green onions

Cut bacon in small pieces. Fry bacon until crisp. Add chopped onions then add hominy and fry for ten minutes. Pepper to taste.

Hominy Soup

4 strips bacon, diced
1/2 cup chopped onion
1 cup boiled hominy
2 cups buttermilk
Salt and pepper to taste
1 tbsp fresh dill chopped

In heavy saucepan fry bacon until tender, pour off excess drippings and add onion. Sauté until golden, add hominy and stir for 5 minutes. Remove pan from stove and add buttermilk, salt and pepper, stirring constantly. Replace on stove and reheat for 5 minutes, carefully stirring and not allowed to boil. Sprinkle with dill and serve.

Hominy with Rotel

1 onion, chopped
1 slice bacon, browned
2 cans golden hominy
1 can Rotel tomatoes
Grated cheese

Brown bacon and crumble into skillet. Add chopped onion and sauté until onion is lightly browned. Add hominy and Rotel and simmer on low heat for 30 minutes. Sprinkle on cheese and heat until cheese melts. Serve hot.

Hominy Casserole

4 slices bacon, browned and crumbled
1 large onion, chopped
1 green pepper, chopped
1 large can mushroom pieces
1 lib. Can hominy, drained
1 can Rotel tomatoes
2 tsp Worcestershire sauce
3 cups grated Cheddar cheese

4 Fry bacon, crumble and set aside. Sauté onion in bacon drippings until golden brown. Mix bacon, onion, green pepper, mushroom pieces, hominy, tomatoes, Worcestershire sauce, salt, and pepper in large mixing bowl. Put layer of mixture in casserole, cover with grated cheese, and repeat until casserole is filled. Bake at 350° for 20 minutes.

Pumpkins & Squash

Pumpkins and squash were some of the first foods to be regularly cultivated by the Cherokee. Drying food for the winter was about the only way to preserve the food. Here is a method passed down directly from a Tribal Elder from the old way.

Dried Pumpkin

Take a ripe pumpkin and cut into horizontal rings. You will need to judge the thickness of the rings, that they will support themselves. This may take some experimentation, so start with 2 inch rings until you've learned more. Remove the rind. Hang on a clean stick in the sun or near a fire. Store until ready for use.

Dried Winter Squash

Peel the squash with a sharp knife. Cut in half and scrape out seeds and pulp. Let dry in sun for two or three days until they can be cut into spiral strips. Hang strips in sun until they are dry.

Cream of Pumpkin Soup

3 cups pumpkin puree
1 large onion, finely minced
3 tbsp butter
6 cups chicken stock or broth
salt & pepper to taste
1/8 tsp nutmeg
1/8 tsp turmeric
1 cup heavy cream

Sauté onions in butter until tender. Place onions and pumpkin in soup pot, add seasonings. Over low heat gradually add stock, stirring until mixture is smooth. Add cream while stirring to blend. Simmer 5 minutes and serve.

Pumpkin Bread

4 eggs
3 cups sugar
1/2 tsp cloves
1 tsp cinnamon
1 tsp nutmeg
1 cup vegetable oil
1 tsp 1/2 salt
1 cup canned pumpkin
2/3 cup water
2 tsp baking soda
3 cups flour

Mix eggs, sugar, cloves, cinnamon, nutmeg oil, and salt thoroughly. Add water, baking soda and flour, mix well. Bake in greased pan at 350° for 1 hour.

Pumpkin Soup

3 medium leeks, white part only, finely chopped
1/2 cup & 2 tsp butter
1 1/3 cups cooked pumpkin
3 large potatoes, peeled and thinly sliced
bouquet garnish (1/2 tsp thyme, 1 tbsp parsley, 1 bay leaf crushed all tied in a bundle of cheese cloth)
4 cups chicken broth
1 1/2 tsp salt
1/2 tsp fresh ground black pepper
1/8 tsp nutmeg
3 cups hot milk
1/2 lb. fresh spinach, Cleaned and chopped
1/2 cup grated Parmesan cheese.

In a large heavy pan sauté chopped leeks in 4 tbsp butter until golden. Add the pumpkin, potatoes, bouquet, 3 cups chicken broth, salt, pepper and nutmeg. Mix well. Bring to a boil and then cook over moderate heat for 1/2 hour, stirring frequently. Remove bouquet, and then puree the mixture. Return to pan, add hot milk and bring to a boil. Reduce heat to low and cook 20 minutes longer, stirring frequently. Meanwhile, cook and drain spinach. Melt 2 tbsp butter and sauté spinach on low heat. Add spinach and remaining broth to pumpkin mixture. Mix well. Remove from heat. Add remaining butter and Parmesan cheese

Baked Pumpkin

1 small pumpkin
2 tbsp apple cider
2 tbsp honey
2 tbsp melted butter

Place washed pumpkins on pie pan and bake at 350° for 1 ½ hours. Remove from oven and cut hole in the top of the pumpkin about 3" to 4" in diameter, save the top. Scoop out pulp and seeds. Mix the honey, cider and butter thoroughly. Baste honey mixture over the flesh of the pumpkin. Replace top and return to oven for 35 to 40 minutes, basting occasionally. Cut into wedges and serve with honey-cider mixture over each serving.

Cream of Squash Soup

1/4 cup butter
2 tsp vegetable oil
1 large onion, finely chopped
2 cloves garlic, minced
3 lbs. yellow squash, thinly sliced
4 cups chicken broth
1 cup half & half
1 1/2 tsp salt
1/2 tsp white pepper

Sauté onion and garlic in butter and vegetable oil until golden brown. Add squash and broth. Cover and simmer for 20 minutes. Pour contents of skillet into blender and blend until smooth. Return to skillet, add half & half, salt and pepper. Simmer over low heat until thoroughly heated. May be served heated or chilled.

Fried Squash Blossoms

2-3 dozen squash blossoms, picked just before blooming
1 cup milk
1/2 cup vegetable oil
1 tbsp flour
1/8 tsp fresh ground pepper
1 tsp salt

In a jar shake together milk, flour, salt and pepper. Coat blossoms with mixture. Fry in skillet in hot oil until golden brown. Drain on paper towel before serving.

Baked Summer Squash

4 squash
3 tbsp butter
1 cup sour cream
1/4 tsp allspice
1 small can pimentos
1/2 cup grated Swiss cheese
1/4 cup dry sherry
Salt and pepper to taste

Steam squash for 20 minutes, or until barely tender. Cut steamed squash in half and place in buttered baking dish. Melt butter and blend in sour cream, allspice, pimentos, cheese sherry salt and pepper. Stir until smooth and pour mixture over squash. Bake at 350° for 15 minutes. Garnish with paprika and serve.

Party Squash

1 lb. squash, sliced
1 tsp sugar
1/2 cup mayonnaise
1/2 cup onion, minced
1/4 cup green pepper, chopped
1/2 cup pecans, chopped
1 egg, slightly beaten
1/2 cup grated cheese
Salt & pepper to taste
Bread crumbs
1/2 stick butter

Steam squash for 20 minutes, drain and mash. Add sugar, mayonnaise, onion, green pepper, pecans, egg, cheese, salt and pepper. Place mixture in 2 qt. casserole and top with bread crumbs and slabs of butter. Bake at 350° for 35 to 40 minutes.

Kanati The Game Hunter

Kanati, was the husband of Selu, the Mother of Corn. Kanati and Selu had two sons, one of which was a "wild boy". He was not naturally born. But sprang from the blood of a deer as Selu washed the meat in the river He had some magical powers but was mostly mischievous.

Now Kanati regularly headed to the woods, soon to return with a big buck, some squirrels and a rabbit or two.

The "wild boy talked his brother into spying on their Father on his next hunting trip to find his secret for always finding game for supper. As Kanati left the next morning the two boys secretly followed him. As they hid and watched, Kanan stopped by a big rock. As he rolled it aside it revealed the opening of a cave and suddenly a big buck shot out. Kanati was ready with his bow and shot him clean. Kanati then rolled the stone back over the cave, slung the buck over his shoulder and headed home.

Now the "wild boy" being even more curious, rushed over to the stone and rolled it aside to look in the cave. When he did a big buck sprang out, then more came. Then out came bears, elk, rabbit's squirrels and all kinds of animals. "Wild boy and his brother just stood by and watched.

Kanati was nearly home when he heard all the noise. It sounded like thunder. He returned to the cave to find the boys and saw that all the animals had escaped from the came. From that day the people had to learn to hunt the game as it roamed the forest.

Wild Rice Soup and Vegetables

60 oz. beef stock or bouillon
4 oz. wild rice
1 lg. onion, finely chopped
1 small potato, finely chopped
1/2 cup carrot, grated
1/2 cup celery, chopped
1 cup mushrooms, sliced
salt and pepper to taste

Heat beef stock in soup pot. Add rice, onion, potato, carrots, celery, salt and pepper. Bring to a boil, and then simmer for 25 minutes. Add more stock or water if necessary. Sauté mushrooms in butter then add to soup and simmer 10-15 minutes longer.

Cabbage Soup

1/2 lb. salt pork
1 cup onion, chopped
4 carrots, peeled and chopped
2 white turnips, sliced
1 head cabbage
3 potatoes, peeled and cubed

Add salt pork to 2 quarts water and simmer for 30 minutes. Add onion, carrots, turnips and simmer for 1 hour. Cut cabbage into quarters and blanch 10 minutes in boiling water. Drain, rinse and slice thinly. Add cabbage to soup, simmer for 30 minutes, and then add potatoes. Simmer until potatoes are tender.

Cream of Cucumber Soup

2 tbsp butter
1/2 cup onion, chopped
1 carrot, sliced
4 cups celery, chopped with leaves
3 cucumbers, peeled and diced
1/4 tsp. thyme
1/2 tsp. tarragon
6 cups chicken broth
2 eggs
1 cup heavy cream
2 tbsp. dry sherry
1/8 tsp. lemon juice
paprika
Toasted sesame seeds

Sauté onion, carrot, and celery in butter until tender. Add cucumbers, thyme, tarragon and broth. Simmer until vegetables are soft. Place mixture in blender and blend until smooth. Return mixture to clean pot and heat. In mixing bowl, beat eggs with cream, sherry and lemon juice. Gradually add 1 cup heated soup to egg mixture, stirring constantly to avoid curdling. Slowly add egg mixture to soup, stirring until well blended Salt and pepper to taste. Serve garnished with paprika and sesame seeds.

Cherokee Pecan Soup

3 1/2 lbs. stewing chicken
3 qts. water
1 onion, chopped
1 cup chopped pecans
Salt and pepper to taste
1 tbsp. fresh dill, minced

Combine chicken, water and onion in soup pot. Bring to a boil, reduce heat and simmer for 3 to 4 hours. Remove chicken from pot and allow cooling enough to remove skin and bones. Break meat into small pieces and return to pot. Add pecans and simmer for 10 minutes. Season to taste with salt, pepper and dill.

Oatmeal Soup

1 1/3 cups oats
1/2 cups butter
1 large onion
3 cloves garlic, minced
2 large tomatoes, chopped
50 oz. chicken broth
1 tsp. salt

Toast oats in heavy skillet over medium heat, stirring, until they just turn brown. Set aside. Melt butter in soup pot, add onions and simmer until onions are tender. Add oats and remaining ingredients. Boil for 6 minutes over medium heat, serve hot.

Black Bean Soup

1 lb. black beans
4 tbsp. bacon drippings
3 large onions, chopped
2 cloves garlic, minced
4 canned tomatoes, drained and crushed
1 tsp. oregano
1/2 tsp. ground cumin
1/4 tsp. thyme
1/8 tsp. marjoram
1 bay leaf
Pinch of ground coriander
3 ham hocks, split in half
1 qt. beef stock
1/3 cup dry sherry
Salt and fresh ground pepper
4 tbsp. wine vinegar

Soak beans overnight covered with cold water or bring beans to a boil, turn off heat and let stand covered for 2 hours. After soaking, bring beans to a boil, reduce heat and simmer for 2 hours, or until beans are tender. Sauté onions and garlic in bacon drippings. Add tomatoes and seasonings to onions and boil 3 minutes. Add onion mixture and ham hocks to beans. Stir in sherry salt and pepper. Cover and simmer for about 2 hours. Remove ham hocks from beans and trim the fat from ham. Break meat into bite-size chunks and place back in soup. Reheat and stir in vinegar. Serve with garnish.

Cherokee Pepper Pot Soup

1 lb. beef short ribs

2 qts. water

2 large onions, quartered

2 ripe tomatoes, seeded and diced

1 large sweet bell pepper, seeded and diced

1 cup okra

1/2 cup potatoes, diced

1/2 cup carrots, sliced

1/2 cup corn

1/4 cup celery, chopped

Salt and ground pepper to taste

Place ribs, water and onions in soup pot. Bring to a boil, then reduce heat and simmer for 3 hours. Remove meat from pot and allow to cool until bones can be removed. Return meat and remaining vegetables to pot and simmer for another 1 1/2 hours. Salt and pepper to taste.

Fish Soup

3 lbs. fish, any kind, filleted

1 1/2 cups course corn meal

1/2 cup wild onions (or fresh greens)

Boil fish in soup pot until tender. Gradually add Corn meal, stirring constantly until desired thickness is reached. Add onions or greens and simmer for 5 minutes.

Turkey Bone Soup

1 chicken or turkey carcass with some meat
2 onions, chopped
3 stalks celery, chopped
1/2 cup rice
6 oz. can tomato sauce
salt and pepper to taste

Cover carcass with cold water in soup pot, bring to a boil and cook until meat falls from bones. Remove bones; add onion, celery, rice, tomato sauce, salt and pepper. Simmer until rice is done.

Peanut Soup

2 cups peanuts, finely chopped, or 1 cup chunky-style peanut butter
2 cups chicken broth
2 cups milk
2 tsp. fresh chives
salt and pepper to taste

Combine peanuts, broth and milk in heavy saucepan. Cook over medium heat 15 minutes, stirring occasionally. Salt and pepper to taste and serve garnished with chives.

Mushroom and Potato Soup

6 tbsp. butter
1 1/2 lbs. fresh mushrooms, cut into 1/8 inch slices, lengthwise
1 cup onions, chopped
6 cups chicken stock
1 1/2 lbs small potatoes, about 6 potatoes, peeled and sliced into 1/4 inch slices
1 tsp. salt
1/4 cup celery, finely chopped
1/4 cup scallions, finely chopped
along with green tops
2 tbsp. sour cream
1 tbsp. dill leaves, chopped finely
fresh ground black pepper

Melt 4 tbsp. butter in a heavy 4-5 quart pot. Add mushrooms and onions and stir until well coated with butter. On low heat simmer mushrooms for 20 minutes Stir in chicken stock, potato slices, and salt. Bring to a boil, then lower heat and simmer for another 25 minutes. Melt remaining 2 tbsp. butter in an 8-10 inch skillet; add celery, scallions and parsley. Cook over low heat, stirring frequently, for 15 minutes or until celery is tender.

Combine sour cream and 1/2 cup simmering mushroom stock and mix well, pour mixture over celery, bring to a boil. Then add celery mixture to soup. Salt and pepper to taste.

Potato Soup

6-8 white potatoes, peeled and sliced

3 medium onions, sliced

1 1/2 tsp. salt

6 cups milk, scalded

2 tbsp. chopped parsley

black pepper

Cover potatoes and onions with cold water in soup pot, add salt. Bring to a boil, lower heat and simmer for 20 minutes. Add milk, pepper and simmer for another 10 minutes... Serve garnished with parsley.

Cream of Cauliflower Soup

1/2 cup butter

1 medium clove garlic, minced

1 large white onion, sliced

1 large head cauliflower, diced

42 oz. chicken broth (3 14 oz. cans)

28 oz. water (2 cans from chicken broth)

1/4 cup half & half

Salt an'd pepper to taste

Sauté onion and garlic until onion is translucent. Add cauliflower, broth and water. Cover and simmer until cauliflower is soft. Let cool, then blend in blender until smooth. Add half & half, salt and pepper. Heat to serve.

Mint and Nut Soup

20 oz. beef broth
1/2 cup raw pinion nuts leaves of 2 stalks mint, washed
2 lib. 4 oz. cans chick peas, drained and rinsed
3 cups water
Fresh ground pepper

Place broth, water and pinion nuts in soup pot and bring to a boil. Reduce heat, add chick peas and simmer 15 minutes. Turn off heat, add mint leaves and let steep 1 minute. Serve seasoned with black pepper.

Tortilla Soup

6 cups chicken broth
12 corn tortillas cut into strips
2 medium tomatoes
1/3 medium onion
1 clove garlic
Grated Monterey Jack cheese
jalapeno pepper

Puree tomatoes, onion and garlic. In soup pot, cook puree in 1 tbsp oil over high flame, stirring. Add broth and salt. Reduce heat and simmer. Heat 1/2 inch oil and fry tortilla strips until they begin to stiffen. Serve soup in bowls then add tortilla strips and cheese. Serve jalapeno pepper on the side.

Mock Turtle Soup

1 qt. beef broth
5 cups water
2 lbs. veal neck bones
1 large veal shank

1 large leek, cleaned and chopped
2 carrots, sliced
2 large stalks celery and leaves, chopped
2 onions
3 parsley sprigs
8 peppercorns
1/2 tsp. marjoram
1 bay leaf
2 cloves garlic
2 cups tomato puree
dash of Tabasco
1/4 cup butter
1/2 cup flour
1 lemon, thinly sliced
salt to taste

Combine first fifteen ingredients in large soup pot, bring to a boil, skim, reduce heat and simmer for 2 hours, or until meat is tender. Remove meat and bones, allow to cool until cool enough to handle. Remove meat and dice. Strain the soup. In a clean pot, melt butter and whisk in flour until smooth and bubbling. Keep stirring until lightly browned. Add the strained soup and bring to a boil, stirring to keep it smooth. Add the meat and simmer. You may add the sliced lemons now or serve them on the side later.

Cherokee Bean Balls

2 cups Brown Beans
4 cups corn meal
1/2 cup flour
1 tsp. soda

Boil beans in plain water until tender. Put corn meal, flour and soda in large mixing bowl. Mix well. Add boiling beans and some of the juice to the corn meal mixture to form a stiff dough. Roll in balls and drop in pot of boiling hot water. Let cook for 30 minutes at slow boil.

Fried Tomato Pones

2 cups green or ripe tomatoes, peeled, seeded, and diced
1 cup corn meal
Salt and pepper to taste
Corn oil for frying

Place tomatoes in mixing bowl, season with salt and pepper. Add corn meal and form into 8 pones or patties. Fry pones in corn oil in large skillet over medium heat for 2 to 3 minutes on each side until golden.

Wild Rice Casserole

1 cup wild rice

3 cups boiling water

2 cans cream of chicken soup

1 can consommé

1 can water

1 bay leaf, crumbled

pinch of thyme

lots of fresh parsley

1/4 tsp. each celery salt, paprika, onion salt, pepper, garlic salt and Accent poultry seasoning

1/2 tsp salt

6 tbsp. onion

4 tbsp. oil

1 1/2 lbs. hamburger

1/2 cup toasted almonds

Pour boiling water over rice and let stand for 15 minutes. Drain, add next 8 ingredients. Brown onions in oil, add meat to onions and brown. Combine with other mixture and refrigerate overnight. Pour into 2 1/2 qt. casserole, sprinkle with nuts and bake at 350° for 3 hours. Keep covered until last 45 minutes, remove cover to brown.

Leather Britches

Leather Britches gets its name from the "look" of tender young beans as they hang to dry. They look like britches hanging on a clothesline. They were dried and stored for the winter. Prepare leather britches by using tender young green beans harvested in the summer, snapping or cutting off the ends and stung through with heavy thread, then dried in the sun for about two months. To cook, wash beans thoroughly, then in a soup pot, soak in cold water for about an hour. Add salt pork, black pepper and bring to a boil, reduce heat and simmer for 3 hours, stirring occasionally, until beans are tender. Salt and pepper to taste.

Herbed Tomatoes

1/4 cup butter
1 tsp brown sugar
1/2 tsp. salt
Black pepper to taste
5 firm tomatoes, peeled
2 tbsp. parsley, chopped
2 tbsp. cloves, chopped
1/2 tsp. oregano
1/4 cup celery, chopped

In deep skillet, melt butter; add sugar, salt and pepper. Add tomatoes, cored side down, cover and cook gently 5 minutes. Carefully, turn tomatoes and add remaining ingredients. Cook uncovered 5 more minutes, basting tomatoes with sauce occasionally. Serve hot with sauce spooned over tomatoes.

Wild Greens

Several wild greens may be prepared in the following manner. These include; wild lettuce, tops of wild beets, dandelions, cochanna, thistle, lambsquarter, deer tongue, sour dock and wild mustard. These should be gathered in the early spring when the leaves are still tender. They may be cooked separately or combined. Wash the leaves well, place in saucepan and cover with water. Boil for 15-20 minutes and drain thoroughly. Fry in oil until tender.

Wilted greens make a healthy and easy salad. For wilted lettuce, watercress or wild onions wash about 1 lb. of greens and shake off as much water as possible. Place in salad bowl and pour 3-4 tbsp. of hot bacon grease over greens. Salt to taste and serve hot.

Poke, Wild Onions & Other Wild Greens

Poke is one of the most popular wild greens among the Oklahoma Cherokee. Poke should be gathered only in the spring because only the young shoots can be eaten. The roots, berries and mature plant contain poison. But if the shoots are cut regularly the greens may be gathered several times from the same spot. Poke should be washed then boiled over high heat for a few minutes. The water should be drained off and discarded. Into a clean soup pot add poke, fresh water salt and bacon drippings.

Wild greens are rich in vitamins and minerals. Wild onions are also a favorite for those who gather them. A favorite use of wild onions is in combination with scrambled eggs. The particular recipe varies with each individual or family. Some like lots of wild onions with only enough scrambled eggs to hold them together. Others prefer to have their scrambled eggs flavored with a small amount of the onions for taste. To cook wild onions with eggs, chop onions into small pieces. Add 2-3 tbsp. bacon drippings or oil in a skillet over medium heat. Add onions, 1/4 cup water and salt to taste, simmer and stir until onions are tender. When most of the water is cooked out and the onions are tender add 6 slightly beaten eggs and scramble. Serve hot with fry bread and honey.

Garlic Tomato

3 small tomatoes

1 clove garlic, mashed

toast

3/4 cup mayonnaise

Peel and slice tomatoes. Cut toast into rounds to fit tomato slices. Put a slice of tomato on each toast round. Mix mayonnaise with garlic and spread on tomatoes. Broil under moderate heat for 3 minutes or until brown and bubbly.

Sweet Potato Cakes

4 large sweet potatoes

3 eggs

1 1/2 tsp salt

1/8 tsp fresh ground pepper

1 tsp soda

Boil sweet potatoes until tender. When cool peel potatoes and mash them in mixing bowl. Add eggs, salt and pepper, mixing into a smooth batter. Heat oiled griddle. Drop batter onto hot griddle from large spoon. Brown on both sides, flattening with spatula, to make cakes about 3"to 4" in diameter. Serve hot with butter.

Baked Sweet Potatoes

Wash sweet potatoes and coat with oil or butter. Place in baking dish and bake at 400° for 1 hour, or until tender. Serve with butter and honey.

Cherokee Mixit

1 lb eggplant, sliced
1 lb zucchini, sliced
1 lb ripe tomatoes, peeled and seeded
1 lb sweet bell peppers, seeded and sliced
1 lb onions, peeled and sliced
1 clove garlic, minced
3 tbsp vegetable oil
3 tbsp vinegar
2 tsp sugar
1 1/2 tsp salt
1/2 tsp fresh ground pepper
Tabasco to taste

In large mixing bowl, toss vegetables with oil, vinegar and sugar. Place vegetables in large soup pot and add salt, pepper and Tabasco. Place over high heat until oil begins to sizzle, and then reduce heat to medium low. Cover and simmer for 1 hour, until vegetables are tender. Serve hot or cold.

Tomato Soup Salad

1 can tomato soup
1 pkg. lemon Jell-O
1 cup mayonnaise
1 cup carrots, grated
1 cup celery, minced
1/2 cup olives

Heat soup, Jell-O and mayonnaise. Let set slightly, add vegetables and pour into glass casserole. Refrigerate until set. Garnish with olives.

Mayan Salad

2 qts. crisp greens in bite size pieces
1 1/2 cups sliced water chestnuts
1 medium mild red onion, thinly sliced
1 grapefruit
2 oranges
1/2 lb cherry tomatoes, halved
cumin dressing
1 large avocado

Mix greens and water chestnuts in large salad bowl. Place onion rings on top of greens. Peel grapefruit and oranges removing white membrane, section and place on onion rings. Arrange tomatoes on top. Cover and chill 1-2 hours. To serve, peel, pit and slice avocado and arrange on top of salad. Pour cumin dressing over salad and toss gently.

Cumin Dressing

3 tbsp cider vinegar
2 tbsp fresh lime juice
6 tbsp salad oil
1 clove garlic
1 tsp cracked black pepper
1/2 tsp salt
1/2 tsp cumin
cayenne pepper to taste

Combine all ingredients in blender until thoroughly blended.

Spinach Salad with Chutney Dressing

1 lb fresh spinach, trimmed of stems, washed and dried
6 mushrooms, sliced
1 cup water chestnuts, sliced
6 slices bacon, cooked crisp, crumbled
3/4 fresh bean sprouts
1/2 cup shredded Gruyere cheese
1/4 cup red onion, thinly sliced

Ingredients should be prepared, and refrigerated separately, a day before serving to maintain crispness. To serve toss all ingredients and cover with chutney dressing.

Chutney Dressing

1/4 cup wine vinegar
2-3 tbsp chutney
1 clove garlic, mashed
2 tbsp coarse ground French mustard
2 tsp. sugar
1/2 cup vegetable oil
Salt and fresh ground pepper to taste

Blend all ingredients in blender until smooth. Season to taste, adjusting oil or chutney as necessary. Refrigerate until needed. Let stand at room temperature for 30 minutes before adding to salad.

Hot Green Bean Salad

1 can green beans
4 strips bacon, sliced
1 cup onion, sliced
1/2 tsp salt
1/8 tsp pepper
1/4 cup vinegar
2 cups potatoes, cooked and diced
2 tbsp pimento, minced

Drain beans, setting aside 1/4 cup liquid. Fry bacon until' crisp, set aside. Add onion to bacon drippings and sauté until tender. Add vinegar, bean liquid, salt and pepper to onions, simmer. Add beans, potatoes and pimento, heat to serving temperature. Crumble bacon over all and serve.

Fried Okra Salad

4 cups okra, washed, drained and sliced
1 medium onion, chopped
1 large ripe tomato, chopped
1 bell pepper, chopped
1 tbsp flour
1/2 cup corn meal

Mix corn meal and flour thoroughly and place in large plastic bag. Place okra in bag and shake until thoroughly coated. Fry okra slowly in hot oil until golden brown. **Toss** okra with chopped vegetables and serve immediately.

Black-eyed Pea Salad

5-15oz cans black-eyed peas
1 cup olive oil
1/2 cup vegetable oil
1/4 cup lemon juice, freshly squeezed
1/2 cup red wine vinegar
5 cloves garlic, minced
10 whole leeks, cleaned, chopped, blanched and drained
1/2 cup fresh parsley, finely chopped
3/4 cups pimentos, chopped
4 medium white onions, thinly sliced
salt and pepper to taste

Drain peas and place in salad bowl. In mixing bowl whisk oils, lemon juice, vinegar and garlic thoroughly. Pour mixture over peas, add remaining ingredients and toss thoroughly. Refrigerate overnight.

Cucumber Salad

1 pkg lime Jell-O
1 1/2 cups hot water
2 tbsp vinegar
1/4 tsp salt
1 tbsp onion, minced
1 cup cucumber, peeled, minced
1/3 cup mayonnaise

Dissolve Jell-O in hot water, add vinegar and salt. Cool until slightly thickened. Beat until fluffy, mix in remaining ingredients and refrigerate until firm.

Tossed Fresh Fruit Salad

1 honey dew melon
1 pineapple
1 pint strawberries
2 oranges
1/2 head crisp lettuce
1 head Romaine

Cut melon in half, remove seeds, peel and cut into bite-size pieces. Chill. Slice off top of pineapple, slice lengthwise into eighths, remove rind and core, cube and chill. Wash and half strawberries, chill. Peel and section oranges. Greens should be crisped in refrigerator, tear greens into bite-size pieces in salad bowl. Add fruit and toss with Orange Mayonnaise Dressing.

Orange Mayonnaise Dressing

1/3 cup honey
3/4 cup mayonnaise
1/4 cup orange juice
1/8 tsp grated onion

Combine honey and mayonnaise. Add juice and onion and mix.

Watercress Salad

In salad bowl mix 1 bunch of watercress with a chopped hard-boiled egg and chopped onion. Add pieces of ham or crumbled bacon. Add favorite salad dressing and toss.

Cole Slaw

1 medium head cabbage
1 medium red onion, sliced and separated into rings
7/8 cup sugar
1 cup vinegar
1 tsp dry mustard
3/4 cup salad oil
1 tsp celery salt
2 tbsp sugar
1 tsp salt

Shred cabbage and onion rings into salad bowl. Sprinkle sugar over cabbage. Heat vinegar, mustard, salad oil, celery salt, sugar and salt. Pour hot mixture over cabbage, let stand 4-6 hours at room temperature. Then stir and refrigerate.

Red Onion Marinade

2 tbsp lemon juice
1/4 cup vegetable oil
1/2 tsp salt
1/8 tsp cracked pepper
1 small red onion thinly sliced and ringed.

Combine all ingredients in mixing bowl, let stand 1/2 hour. Serve over tomato wedges.

Dill Pickle Salad

2 pkg plain gelatin,
soften in 1 cup water and set aside
1 cup sugar
1/4 tsp salt
1/4 cup lemon juice
1/2 cup dill pickle juice
1/4 cup pimento juice
1/4 cup pineapple juice
2 medium dill pickles, finely chopped
1/2 cup pimento, chopped
1 cup pineapple, crushed
1 cup nuts, chopped

Bring sugar, salt and juices to a boil, stir into softened gelatin until gelatin is melted. Chill until mixture begins to thicken. Stir pickle, pimento, pineapple and nuts into gelatin and refrigerate.

Poppy Seed Dressing

1 1/2 cups sugar
2 tsp dry mustard
3 tsp salt
2/3 cup vinegar
3 tbsp onion juice
2 cups salad oil - not olive oil
3 tbsp poppy seeds

Mix sugar, mustard, salt and vinegar. Add onion juice and stir thoroughly. Add oil slowly, whisking until thick. Add poppy seeds and whisk thoroughly. Refrigerate. Serve over fresh fruit.

Spoon Bread

1 # 300 can cream style corn
3/4 cup milk
1/3 cup melted shortening or oil
3 eggs, slightly beaten
1 1/2 cup yellow corn meal
1/2 tsp baking powder
1 tsp salt
1 tsp sugar
1 1/2 cup grated cheese
14 oz can chop green chile

Combine corn, milk, oil, eggs, corn meal baking powder, salt and sugar. Mix to a batter. Place 1/2 mixture in greased 9"x 9" bread pan. Put 1/2 cheese and chilies on batter. Place remaining batter over cheese and chilies. Cover with remaining cheese and chilies. Bake at 400° for 45 minutes.

Buttermilk Biscuits

1 1/2 cups buttermilk
3/4 cup warm water
2 pkgs yeast
6 tsp sugar
3 tsp baking powder
pinch of salt
5 cups flour

Dissolve yeast in water. Mix flour, sugar, baking soda and salt. Add buttermilk and yeast. Blend thoroughly and knead. Shape into balls and let rise 1-1 1/2 hours. Bake at 400° for 20-30 minutes until brown.

Cherokee Fry Bread

1 Cup flour
1/2 tsp salt
2 tsp baking powder
3/4 cup milk

Mix ingredients in mixing bowl, adding more flour if necessary to make stiff dough. Roll dough out on floured board until very thin. Cut into strips 2x3 inches and drop in hot deep fat fryer. Brown on one side, turn, and brown on other side. Remove from fryer and place on paper towels to absorb oil.

Fry Bread

2 cups self-rising flour
1 1/2 cups milk or buttermilk
2 tbsp sugar

Place flour in large bowl; add milk and sugar, mix into stiff dough. Prepare shortening in deep fat fryer and heat to 400°. Place dough on floured board and roll to 1/2" thickness. Cut into desired shape and drop into hot oil. When one side has turned golden brown, turn and brown other side. Drain on paper towels. Serve hot with honey.

Indian Herb Dressing

1/4 cup sugar
3 tbsp water
2 tbsp honey
1/4 cup tomato juice
1 tsp minced dried onion
1 tsp minced dried parsley
2/3 cup oil
Sweet basil
Rose hips
Saffron
Horseradish
Sorrel
Mustard
Wild chia
Sesame seeds

Blend vinegar, water, honey, tomato juice, onion and parsley. Add a pinch each of sweet basil, rose hips, saffron, horseradish, sorrel, mustard and wild chia. Let stand overnight. Toss with salad and sprinkle with sesame seeds.

Cold Beef Salad

1/4 cup red wine vinegar
1/4 cup water
2 tbsp lemon juice
2 tbsp sugar
1/4 tsp dill weed
1/2 tsp salt
Fresh ground pepper to taste
3 cups cold beef cut into strips
1 small red onion, thinly sliced
1 head Romaine lettuce
1 cup sour cream
tomato wedges

Simmer vinegar, water, lemon juice, sugar, dill weed, salt and pepper over low heat for 15 minutes. Cool, combine with beef and onion and chill several hours. Drain and **save** liquid. Tear lettuce in large salad bowl. Top with beef and onion. Combine sour cream with saved liquid, mix well and pour over beef. Toss and serve.

Fried Green Tomatoes

Slice green or half ripened tomatoes. Salt and pepper to taste. Coat with flour and fry in hot oil in skillet until browned.

Fried Mushrooms

Soak mushrooms overnight in salt water. Salt and pepper to taste. Coat with flour and fry in hot oil in skillet until browned. Serve hot.

Sourdough Biscuits

1 cup sourdough starter

1 tsp salt

1 tsp sugar

1 tsp soda

1 tbsp shortening

3-4 cups flour

Place flour in mixing bowl, make a well in center and add sourdough starter. Stir in salt, sugar and soda. Add shortening. Add flour to make stiff dough. Pinch of dough, one biscuit at a time, form a ball and roll in melted shortening. Place biscuits, crowed, in a pan and let rise 20-30 minutes. Bake at 425° until browned.

Sourdough Starter

2 cups lukewarm potato water

2 cups flour

1 tbsp sugar

Boil 2 cut up potatoes in 3 cups water until tender. Remove potatoes and measure 2 cups of remaining liquid. Mix potato water, flour and sugar into a smooth paste. Set in a warm area until starter mixture rises to double.

Chestnut Bread

Peel 1 lb of chestnuts and scale to take off inside skin. Add enough corn meal to hold chestnuts together, mixing chestnuts and corn meal with boiling water. Wrap in green corn shucks, tying each with twine. Place in a pot of boiling water and cook until done.

Carrot Bread

1 lb carrots, peeled and grated

1 1/4 cups milk

1 1/4 cups unbleached flour

1 1/4 cups corn meal

1 1/2 tsp baking powder

2 eggs, beaten

2 tbsp melted butter

1/2 cup honey

1/2 cup dried blueberries or raisins

Preheat oven to 375°. Place carrots in saucepan, add milk and bring to a boil. Reduce heat and simmer for 5 minutes, stirring occasionally. Remove from heat and allow to cool. In a mixing bowl, combine flour, corn meal, baking powder, eggs, butter and honey. Stir in dried blueberries or raisins, carrots and milk. Butter a large loaf pan. Pour batter into pan and bake for 1 hour, until a knife inserted into the bread comes out clean.

Cherokee Huckleberry Bread

2 cups self-rising flour

1 cup sugar

1 cup milk

2 cups berries (huckleberries or blueberries)

1 egg

1 stick butter

1 tsp vanilla extract

Cream eggs, butter and sugar together. Add flour, milk and vanilla. Sprinkle flour on berries to prevent them from sinking in batter. Add berries to mixture. Put in baking pan and bake at 350° about 40 minutes.

Bean Bread

2 cups corn meal
1 tsp salt
1 tsp baking powder
2 eggs
1 1/2 cups milk
2 cups cooked pinto beans, drained

Mix dry ingredients thoroughly, add milk and eggs. Stir in beans and pour into greased pan. Bake at 450° for 20 minutes or until brown.

Blue Corn Muffins

1 1/2 cups flour
1 cup blue corn meal
3 tsp baking powder
1 tsp salt
1 tsp sugar
1 1/2 cups milk
2 eggs, well beaten
1/3 cup cooking oil

Sift flour, corn meal, baking powder, sugar and salt together. Add milk, oil and well beaten eggs. Mix until smooth. Fill well greased muffin pan 3/4 full. Bake at 400° for 20-25 minutes.

Homemade Corn meal Tortillas

1 cup flour
1/2 cup corn meal
1/4 tsp salt
1 egg
1 1/2 cup cold water

Mix all ingredients in mixing bowl. Beat until batter is smooth. Spoon 3 tbsp batter onto hot ungreased griddle. When edges begin to dry, turn over. Bake until dry, not brown.

Persimmon Bread

1 1/2 cups sugar
1/2 tsp cloves
1/2 cup oil
1 tsp salt
2 eggs
1 1/2 tsp nutmeg
1 cup persimmon pulp
1/2 tsp cinnamon
1 3/4 cups flour
1/2 cup raisins
1 tsp soda
1/4 tsp baking powder
1/2 tsp allspice

In mixing bowl, mix oil and water thoroughly. Add eggs, pulp, spices, flour and raisins, mix well. Pour mixture into greased loaf pan. Fill 2/3 full, bake at 350° for 45 minutes.

Blueberry Wild Rice Muffins

3 tbsp butter
1 cup sugar
1/2 cup
water
1/2 cup evaporated milk
2 cups flour
1 tsp salt
1 1/2 cups blueberries
1 cup cooked wild rice

Blend softened butter with sugar. Add water, milk, flour, salt and baking powder. Stir until smooth. Fold in blueberries and wild rice. Pour into well greased muffin pan, bake at 350° for 25 minutes.

Strawberry Bread

3 cups flour
2 cups sugar
3 tsp cinnamon
1 tsp soda
1 tsp salt
1 1/4 cups oil
4 eggs, beaten
2-10 oz boxes frozen strawberries, thawed
1 1/4 cups chopped pecan

Combine dry ingredients. Add oil and eggs, mix well. Add strawberries and pecans. Grease and flour 2 loaf pans. Bake at 350° for 1 1/2 hours.

Bread Stuffing

8 cups bread crumbs
1/2 cup butter
1 cup chopped onion
1 cup celery, chopped with leaves
1 1/2 tsp salt
1/2 tsp Tabasco
1/2 tbsp poultry seasoning
2 tbsp chopped parsley
1/4 cup chicken bullion

Melt butter in saucepan; add onions, celery, Tabasco, poultry seasoning, and salt. Cook onion until tender, not brown. Combine with bread crumbs and parsley. Add bullion, toss lightly with fork until well mixed. Mushroom-Add 1/2 cup canned mushrooms, omit bullion. Corn bread-Substitute 4 cups corn bread for 4 cups bread.

Spoon Bread

2 1/2 cups milk
1/2 cup corn meal
1 tbsp butter
1 tsp baking powder
1 tsp salt
3 eggs, well beaten

Heat 2 cups of milk with corn meal, cook until thickens. Add butter, remaining milk, baking powder, salt and eggs mix thoroughly. Bake in greased pan at 350° for 30-40 minutes.

Chipped Beef in Mushroom Sauce

3/4 lb dried chipped beef
2 cans condensed cream of mushroom soup
1/4 cup butter
2 cups milk
1 tsp Worcestershire sauce
freshly ground pepper
1/2 cup toasted almonds

Soak chipped beef in 2 cups hot water for 2 minutes. Drain and discard water. Sauté beef in butter in chafing dish for 5 minutes, stirring constantly. Combine soup with milk and stir until smooth and thoroughly blended. Stir soup and Worcestershire sauce into beef. Season with pepper and simmer for 10 minutes, stirring occasional. Sprinkle with almonds, serve over toast.

Drip Beef

6-7 lbs Pikes Peak roast
1 bay leaf
1 tbsp pepper
1 tbsp oregano
1 tbsp rosemary
1 tbsp summer savory
1 tbsp garlic powder
1 beef bullion cube

Place all ingredients in soup pot. Cover 1/2 with water, heat to a boil. Salt and pepper to taste. Lower heat and simmer until beef is fork tender. Shred meat just before serving.

Paprika Beef

2 lbs beef round, cut into 1 1/2 inch pieces
2 tbsp flour
1 tsp salt
2 tsp paprika
dash of nutmeg
2 tbsp oil
1 cup beef bullion
1/2 cup sour cream
2 tbsp chopped parsley
package of noodles

Dredge beef in mixture of flour, salt, 1 tsp paprika and nutmeg. Brown meat slowly in hot oil. Add bullion, cover and simmer 2 hours or until tender. Cook noodles according to package directions, drain. Add remaining paprika and sour cream to meat and blend. Arrange noodles on serving dish, cover with meat and sauce. Garnish with parsley.

Venison Steak

Slice steaks about 1/4 inch thick Beat them as for round steak, salt and pepper to taste and roll in flour. Brown in oil, drain fat and cover with water. Simmer for 30 minutes or until water evaporates, serve hot or cold.

Roast Venison

Salt roast and place in saucepan with 2-3 tbsp of shortening. Cover with water and boil 2 hours or until tender. Drain broth and save for other uses. Place roast in baking dish, season with pepper and sage. Bake at 350° for 10 minutes.

Fried Rabbit

Wash and cut rabbit into serving pieces. Place rabbit in soup pot. Cover with water and cook until meat is tender. Remove from pot, flour pieces, salt and fry in a skillet.

Batter Fried Frog Legs

1 egg, beaten
1/2 tsp salt
2 lbs frog legs
1/2 cup corn meal
1/8 tsp pepper
1/2 cup cooking oil

Mix egg, corn meal, salt and pepper into a batter. Dip frog legs in batter and fry in oil in heavy skillet for 25 minutes, turning to brown evenly.

Ceviche

2 lbs fish fillets, any kind with thick firm meat - not catfish or salt fatty fish
1 large sweet onion, cut into ring
1 large bell pepper, cut into rings
juice of 3 fresh limes
Salt and pepper
2 tbsp white wine vinegar

Cut fish fillets into bite size pieces. Place fish, onion, green pepper, salt and pepper in glass casserole dish with lid. Pour lime juice over all; add vinegar to barely cover fish and vegetables. Mix carefully, cover and refrigerate 24 hours.

Herbed Chicken

3 chicken breasts, halved
Flour
Butter
2 cans mushroom soup
3/4 cups sherry
1 5oz can water chestnuts or almonds
1 cup mushrooms, drained
2 tbsp green pepper
1/4 tsp thyme

Season chicken breasts with salt and pepper, flour lightly and brown in butter. Arrange in shallow pan. Add mushroom soup to drippings and heat slowly. Add sherry, water chestnuts or almonds, mushrooms, green pepper and thyme, stir. Pour over chicken and bake at 350° covered for 30 minutes. Uncover and bake 30 more minutes.

Chicken Breast Casserole

3 chicken breasts, halved and skinned
6 slices bacon
2 pkg chipped beef
1 can mushroom soup, undiluted
1/2 pint sour cream

Place dripped beef in bottom of flat baking dish. Wrap each breast with bacon slice and arrange on beef. Mix soup and sour cream, pour over chicken and beef. Bake at 275° for 3 hours uncovered. Occasionally spoon soup mixture over chicken breasts.

Breast of Chicken With Wild Rice

Breasts of 3 lb chickens
1 lh mushrooms, sliced
1/2 cup butter
1 tbsp grated onion
2 cups heavy cream
4 tbsp brandy
4 tbsp dry sherry
1/2 tsp salt
fresh ground pepper
8 oz cooked wild rice

De-bone and skin chicken breasts. Season with salt and pepper. Sauté in butter over low heat for 20 minutes or until brown. Remove chicken and keep hot. Add mushrooms and onions to butter remaining in pan and cook for 5 minutes, stirring constantly. Lower heat and slowly add cream, continuing to stir. Simmer for 5 minutes. Add brandy and sherry and simmer for 5 more minutes. Arrange chicken over wild rice and cover with sauce.

Venison Stew

2 lbs venison chunks
2 cups tomatoes, canned
2 large potatoes
1 small cabbage
2 large onions
1 carrot
1 green pepper
salt to taste

Cover venison with water and boil 1 1/2-2 hours or until meat is tender. Drain broth and place vegetables in broth and simmer on low heat 20 minutes. Add meat to stew and serve.

Country Fried Squirrel

2 squirrels
Salt and pepper to taste
flour to dredge
6 tbsp fat
2 cups water

Cut squirrel into serving pieces. Place flour and seasoning in paper bag, place squirrel in bag and shake until coated. Fry in skillet until golden brown, pour off excess grease and add water. Bring to a boil, lower heat, cover and simmer for 1 hour.

Squirrel Stew

Salt and pepper squirrel to taste. Boil in water until tender. Remove squirrel and de-bone. Place meat back in broth, add a little butter and drop 3-4 eggs into broth. Do not stir until eggs are done.

Hickory Nut Pie

1/2 cup sugar
1/4 cup butter
1 cup butter flavored syrup
1/4 tsp salt
2 eggs
1 cup hickory nuts
1 unbaked pie shell

Beat eggs well, mix sugar and butter, add to eggs and beat together. Add syrup, salt and nuts. Pour into pie shell. Bake at 425° for 15 minutes, lower heat to 350° bake for 45 more minutes.

Baked Indian Pudding

6 cups milk
1/2 cup corn meal
1 1/2 tsp flour
1/2 tsp cinnamon
1/4 tsp ginger
1/4 tsp ground cloves
2 tbsp butter
1 cup molasses

Preheat oven to 300°. In 3 qt saucepan, over medium heat, heat 4 cups milk until very hot but not boiling. In mixing bowl, combine corn meal, flour, cinnamon, ginger, and cloves. Slowly stir mixture into milk, stirring constantly until mixture is very thick, about 15 minutes. Remove from heat and stir in butter until melted. Beat in molasses and remaining milk. Pour into greased 2 qt casserole. Bake at 300° for 3 hours.

Pear Pudding

4 1/2 cups cooked pears, smashed
2 tbsp flour
1/2 cup sugar
1/2 tsp cinnamon
1/2 cup quick oatmeal
1/2 cup sifted flour
1/2 cup brown sugar
1/2 cup softened butter

Combine pears, 2 tbsp flour, sugar and cinnamon, place in buttered baking dish. Combine oatmeal, sifted flour, brown sugar and butter. Pour over pear mixture. Bake at 350° for 45 minutes.

Sweet Potato Pudding

3 large sweet potatoes, grated
1/2 lb sugar
1/2 tsp allspice
4 eggs
1/2 cup butter
1/2 cup milk

Beat eggs and sugar together, add butter and beat to a cream. Add rest of ingredients and bake at 350° for one hour.

Pecan Balls

1 cup butter
3 tbsp powdered sugar
2 cups flour
1 tbsp vanilla
1 cup broken pecans

Beat butter and sugar into smooth cream. Add flour, vanilla and nuts. Form into balls and bake at 250° for 45 minutes. While warm roll balls in powdered sugar.

Baked Apricots

3 large cans apricot halves, drained
1 box light brown sugar
1 large box Ritz crackers
butter

In a greased baking dish, place a layer of apricots. Cover with brown sugar and a layer of crumbled crackers. Dot with butter. Repeat layers to top of dish. Bake at 300° for 1 hour.

Cherokee Persimmon Cake

1 cup persimmon pulp
1/2 cup sugar
1 egg
1 tbsp butter
1 cup flour
1 tsp baking powder
1/2 tsp soda

Combine all ingredients in mixing bowl and mix well. Pour into greased and floured pan and bake at 350° for 40 minutes.

Grape Dumplings

1 cup flour
1 1/2 tsp baking powder
2 tsp sugar
1/4 tsp salt
1 tbsp shortening
1/2 cup grape juice

Mix flour, baking powder, sugar, salt and shortening. Add juice and mix into stiff dough. Roll dough very thin on floured board. Cut into strips 1/2" wide, 2" long. Drop into boiling grape juice, cover and cook for 10-12 minutes.

www.ingramcontent.com/pod-product-compliance
Lightning Source LLC
Chambersburg PA
CBHW021023090426
42738CB00007B/888